MW01206454

Bible Study Lessons
For Kids Ages 8-12

Interactive Journeys into Scripture and Friendship with God

Gilead Publishing

Table of Contents

Introduction

The Bible is like a big treasure chest filled with exciting stories, important lessons, and wisdom from God! For kids like you, the Bible is more than just an old book—it is a guide to help you understand life, make good choices, and grow in your friendship with God.

This book, *Bible Study Lessons for Kids Ages 6-12: Interactive Scriptural Handbook to Grow in Faith and Explore God's Love for Curious Minds*, is here to help you learn about God's amazing stories and how they connect to your life. It is not just about reading—it's about discovering, exploring, and having fun while learning about God's love!

Why This Book?

You are at an exciting stage in life! You are curious, full of questions, and ready to learn. This book is designed just for you!

- You will explore incredible stories from the Bible, from how the world was created to Jesus' amazing miracles.
- You will discover important lessons about kindness, patience, courage, and faith.
- You will learn how to apply what you read to your everyday life.
- You will have fun with activities that help bring the lessons to life!

How Will You Learn?

Each lesson in this book is simple, fun, and interactive. Every lesson will include:

- A Bible Story – A simple and exciting retelling of a story from the Bible.
- Key Lessons – The most important things to remember from the story.
- Life Application – How you can use the lesson in your daily life.
- Reflective Questions – Fun and thoughtful questions to help you think and talk about what you learned.

- A Short Prayer – A simple way to talk to God about what you've learned.

What Is the Most Important Thing?

The most important thing is that God loves you so much! Through these lessons, you will learn how much He cares for you, how He guides you, and how He wants to be your best friend.

Are you ready for this exciting adventure into God's Word? Let's begin!

Lesson 1: The Story of Creation: How God Made the World

Study Scripture: Genesis 1:1-5

The Beginning of Everything

Before anything existed, there was only darkness. No sky, no land, no animals—nothing at all! But God was there, and He had a wonderful plan.

With just His words, God began to create. He said, "Let there be light!" and at that moment, light appeared! The darkness was no longer everywhere. God called the light "day" and the darkness "night."

This was the very first day of creation. It was the beginning of the beautiful world God was making!

Key Lessons

- God is powerful—He can create something out of nothing.
- Light was the first thing God made, showing its importance in His creation.
- God's words are strong and full of life.

Life Application:

Every morning when you wake up and see the sunshine, remember that God created light for us. Just like He made the world full of wonderful things, He also made you special.

God has a purpose for everything He created, including you! Be thankful for His creation and take care of the world around you.

Reflective Questions/Exercises:

1. What is your favorite thing that God created?
2. How does it feel knowing that God made light just by speaking?
3. What can you do each day to thank God for His creation?

Prayer:

Dear God,
 Thank You for creating light and everything in

the world. I am grateful that You made me special, too. Help me to always remember Your power and love. Teach me to care for Your creation and to live in a way that pleases You. Amen.

Lesson 2: God's Special Creation: The Value of People

Study Scripture: Genesis 1:26-27

People Are God's Special Creation

After making the sky, land, sea, plants, and animals, God saved the best for last—people! He wanted to create someone very special, so He made people in His own image.

The Bible says that God said, "Let us make man in our image." That means humans are different from animals—we can think, love, make choices, and have a relationship with God.

God made both men and women, and He gave them an important job—to take care of the world He had created. When He finished, He looked at everything He made and called it very good.

Unlike anything else in creation, people reflect God's love and creativity. That means you are special, important, and deeply loved by God.

Key Lessons:

- People are made in God's image, making us unique and special.

- God gave humans the responsibility to care for the earth.
- God calls us "very good" because we are His special creation.

Life Application:

You are made in God's image! That means you are valuable, loved, and created with a purpose.

When you look at others, remember that they are special too. We should treat people with kindness and respect because everyone is created by God.

And when you ever feel unimportant or unsure of yourself, remember—God made you just the way you are, and He loves you!

Reflective Questions/Exercises:

1. What does it mean to you that you are made in God's image?

2. How can you show kindness to someone, knowing they are special to God too?
3. What are some ways you can help take care of God's creation?

Prayer:

Dear God,

Thank You for making me in Your image. Help me to see how special I am and to treat others with kindness because they are special too. Show me how to take care of the world You made and to love others the way You love me. Amen.

Lesson 3: Noah and the Great Flood: A Story of Faith and Obedience

Study Scripture: Genesis 6:9-22

Noah's Faith and God's Plan

A long time after God created the world, people began to do many bad things. They had forgotten about God and were making wrong choices. But there was one man who still obeyed God—Noah.

Noah loved God and listened to Him, so God gave him a special command. He told Noah to build a big ark (a giant boat) because a great flood was coming. This flood would cover the whole earth to clean away all the evil.

God gave Noah specific instructions on how to build the ark. It had to be huge, with many rooms for animals. Noah trusted God and worked hard to build the boat, even though people around him laughed at him and didn't believe a flood was coming.

When the ark was ready, God told Noah to bring his family and two of every animal into the ark. Then, the rain started falling! It rained for 40 days and 40 nights, covering the earth with water. But Noah and his family were safe inside the ark because they trusted and obeyed God.

Key Lessons:

- Noah trusted God even when others didn't believe.
- God protects those who follow Him.
- Obedience to God brings blessings.

Life Application:

Sometimes, doing the right thing isn't easy. Other people might make fun of you, just like they laughed at Noah. But when you trust and obey God, He will always be with you and take care of you.

When God asks us to follow Him, it might not always make sense at first, but His plans are always good. Just like Noah, we should listen, trust, and obey God even when it's hard.

Reflective Questions/Exercises:

1. How do you think Noah felt when people laughed at him?

2. What can you learn from Noah's obedience to God?
3. Can you think of a time when you had to trust God even when it was difficult?

Prayer:

Dear God,

Thank You for Noah's story, which teaches me to trust and obey You. Help me to listen to You even when others don't. Give me the strength to do what is right and to always follow Your plan. Amen.

Lesson 4: God's Rainbow Promise: A Sign of His Faithfulness

Study Scripture: Genesis 9:12-17

God's Promise to Noah

After the great flood covered the earth, Noah, his family, and all the animals were safe inside the ark. Then, one day, the rain stopped, and the water began to go down.

Noah waited patiently until God told him it was time to leave the ark. When Noah and his family stepped outside, they saw that the world had changed. The land was dry, and a fresh new beginning had started.

The first thing Noah did was thank God for keeping them safe. He built an altar and worshipped God. God was pleased with Noah's faith and made a special promise, called a covenant.

God said, "Never again will I flood the whole earth." As a sign of His promise, He placed a beautiful rainbow in the sky. The rainbow would be a reminder that God keeps His promises and that He is always faithful.

Key Lessons:

- God always keeps His promises.
- The rainbow is a sign of God's love and faithfulness.
- We should always be thankful to God for His protection.

Life Application:

Every time you see a rainbow, remember that God is faithful. Just as He kept His promise to Noah, He keeps His promises to us too.

When you pray or ask God for help, trust that He hears you and will take care of you. Like Noah, we should also be grateful and thank God for all He has done for us.

Reflective Questions/Exercises:

1. What do you think when you see a rainbow?

2. Why is it important to trust that God keeps His promises?
3. How can you show thankfulness to God in your daily life?

Prayer:

Dear God,

Thank You for always keeping Your promises. Every time I see a rainbow, help me to remember Your love and faithfulness. Teach me to trust You and to always be thankful. Amen.

Lesson 5: Abraham's Test of Faith

Study Scripture: Genesis 22:1-14

Abraham's Big Test

Abraham had always followed God and trusted Him. One day, God gave Abraham a difficult command—to offer his son, Isaac, as a sacrifice. This was a test to see if Abraham truly trusted God with everything.

Even though Abraham didn't understand why, he obeyed God. He took Isaac and journeyed up a mountain to do what God had asked. As they walked, Isaac noticed that something was missing. "Father, where is the lamb for the sacrifice?" he asked.

Abraham replied, "God will provide."

Just as Abraham was about to offer Isaac, God stopped him! He saw Abraham's strong faith and provided a ram for the sacrifice instead. Abraham had passed the test—he had proven that he fully trusted God.

Because of his faith, God blessed Abraham and his family for generations to come.

Key Lessons:

- Trusting God means obeying Him even when things don't make sense.
- God provides for His people.
- Faith leads to blessings and a closer relationship with God.

Life Application:

Sometimes, life doesn't go the way we expect, and we may not understand why things happen. But just like Abraham, we should trust that God knows what's best.

Whenever you feel unsure or afraid, remember that God has a plan for you, and He will always take care of you.

Reflective Questions/Exercises:

1. Why do you think God tested Abraham's faith?

2. How do you think Abraham felt during his journey up the mountain?
3. Can you think of a time when you had to trust God, even when it was hard?

Prayer:

Dear God,

Thank You for always providing what I need. Help me to trust You, even when things don't make sense. Give me the courage to follow Your plan and believe that You always take care of me. Amen.

Lesson 6: Jacob's Dream – A Ladder to Heaven

Study Scripture: Genesis 28:10-19

Jacob's Special Dream

Jacob was on a long journey, traveling alone. As night fell, he found a place to sleep, using a stone as his pillow. While he was sleeping, God gave him a special dream.

In his dream, Jacob saw a ladder reaching from earth to heaven, and angels were going up and down on it. At the top of the ladder stood God Himself!

God spoke to Jacob and made a wonderful promise. He told Jacob that his family would grow into a great nation and that He would always be with him.

When Jacob woke up, he knew that God had spoken to him. He set up a stone as a reminder of this special place and named it Bethel, meaning "House of God."

Key Lessons:

- God is always with us, no matter where we are.
- God speaks to us in different ways, even through dreams.

- God has a plan for our lives, just as He did for Jacob.

Life Application:

Sometimes we may feel alone or uncertain about the future, just like Jacob. But this story reminds us that God is always near us and has a plan for our lives.

We don't need to see a ladder to heaven to know that God is always working in our lives and guiding us.

Reflective Questions/Exercises:

1. What do you think Jacob felt when he saw the dream?
2. What does this story teach us about God's presence?
3. Have you ever had a moment where you felt God was near?

Prayer:

Dear God,

Thank You for always being with me, just like You were with Jacob. Help me to trust that You have a plan for my life. Remind me that You are near, even when I can't see You. Amen.

Lesson 7: Joseph's Journey – From a Colorful Coat to a Great Leader

Study Scripture: Genesis 37:3-36

Joseph's Special Gift and His Brothers' Jealousy

Joseph was his father Jacob's favorite son, and to show his love, Jacob gave Joseph a beautiful, colorful coat. This made Joseph's brothers very jealous. They didn't like how much attention Joseph got, and they became angry with him.

Joseph also had strange dreams where he saw himself as a ruler, and his family bowing before him. When he told his brothers about these dreams, they became even more upset.

One day, Joseph's brothers saw him coming and came up with a cruel plan. They took his coat and threw him into a deep pit. Then, instead of leaving him there, they decided to sell him as a slave. They told their father that Joseph had been killed by a wild animal.

Although Joseph went through difficult times, God had a greater plan for him. This was just the beginning of an amazing journey where Joseph would go from being a servant to a great leader.

Key Lessons:

- Jealousy can lead to unkind actions, so we must learn to be happy for others.
- Even when bad things happen, God has a bigger plan for our lives.
- God can turn difficult situations into something good.

Life Application:

Sometimes, life may feel unfair, just like it did for Joseph. But God sees everything and never forgets us. Even when people treat us badly, we should trust God and believe that He is working things out for good.

Instead of feeling jealous, we should learn to be happy when others receive blessings and trust that God has good things in store for us, too.

Reflective Questions/Exercises:

1. How do you think Joseph felt when his brothers treated him badly?
2. Why is it important to be happy for others instead of feeling jealous?
3. Have you ever gone through a difficult situation but later saw that God had a plan?

Prayer:

Dear God,

Thank You for always being with me, even when things don't go my way. Help me to be happy for others and to trust that You have a good plan for my life. Teach me to be kind and patient in every situation. Amen.

Lesson 8: Moses and the Burning Bush – God Calls a Leader

Study Scripture: Exodus 3:1-12

God Speaks to Moses Through Fire

Moses had grown up in Egypt but later lived in the desert as a shepherd. One day, while watching over the sheep, he saw something amazing—a bush that was on fire but not burning up!

As he got closer, a voice called his name—"Moses! Moses!" It was God speaking to him! God told Moses that He had seen how His people, the Israelites, were suffering in Egypt, and He wanted to rescue them.

Then, God gave Moses a very important mission. He told him to go back to Egypt and tell Pharaoh to set the Israelites free.

Moses was afraid. He didn't think he was the right person for the job. "Who am I to do this?" he asked.

But God reassured him, saying, "I will be with you."

Moses didn't feel ready, but God promised to help him every step of the way.

Key Lessons:

- God calls ordinary people to do great things.
- We don't have to be perfect—God gives us the strength we need.
- God is always with us, even when we feel afraid.

Life Application:

Sometimes, God asks us to do things that seem difficult or scary. Maybe it's standing up for what's right, helping someone, or trying something new.

When we feel nervous or unsure, we can trust that God is with us, just like He was with Moses. We don't have to be the strongest or the smartest—God helps us do what we need to do.

Reflective Questions/Exercises:

1. How do you think Moses felt when he saw the burning bush?
2. Why do you think Moses was scared to follow God's instructions?
3. What is something that God might be asking you to do that feels scary?

Prayer:

Dear God,

Thank You for always being with me. Sometimes, I feel afraid or unsure, but I know that You will help me just like You helped Moses. Give me courage to follow Your plans and trust You in every situation. Amen.

Lesson 9: The Ten Commandments – God's Rules for His People

Study Scripture: Exodus 20:1-21

God's Special Rules for His People

After leading the Israelites out of slavery in Egypt, God wanted to teach them how to live as His people. He brought them to Mount Sinai, where He would give them important instructions.

The mountain was covered with thick smoke, loud thunder, and bright lightning. Then, God spoke to Moses and gave him ten important rules, known as the Ten Commandments. These commandments would help the Israelites know how to live in a way that honored God.

The first four commandments were about loving and respecting God:

1. Put God first—Don't worship other gods.
2. Only worship God—Don't make or pray to idols.
3. Respect God's name—Don't use it in a wrong way.
4. Keep the Sabbath holy—Set aside a day to rest and focus on God.

The last six commandments were about how to treat others:

5. Honor your parents—Listen to and respect them.

6. Do not kill—Value every life.

7. Be faithful—Keep your promises.

8. Do not steal—Always be honest.

9. Do not lie—Speak the truth.

10. Do not be jealous—Be happy with what you have.

These commandments weren't just for the Israelites—they are still important for us today!

Key Lessons:

- God gives us rules because He loves us and wants the best for us.
- The Ten Commandments teach us how to love God and others.
- Obeying God's rules helps us live a good and happy life.

Life Application:

Rules aren't meant to stop us from having fun—they are there to protect us and help us make good choices.

When we follow God's commandments, we show Him love and respect. We also learn how to treat others kindly and live in a way that pleases God.

Reflective Questions/Exercises:

1. Why do you think God gave the Israelites the Ten Commandments?
2. Which commandment do you think is the most important?
3. How can you follow God's rules in your everyday life?

Prayer:

Dear God,
Thank You for giving us rules to guide our lives. Help me to follow Your commandments and to

make good choices every day. Teach me to love and respect You and to treat others with kindness. Amen.

Lesson 10: The Red Sea Miracle – God's Power to Rescue

Study Scripture: Exodus 14:1-31

God Makes a Way Through the Sea

After Pharaoh finally let the Israelites leave Egypt, they thought they were free. But soon, they found themselves in big trouble—Pharaoh changed his mind and sent his army after them!

The Israelites were trapped. In front of them was the Red Sea, and behind them was Pharaoh's army. They were afraid and didn't know what to do. But God had a plan.

God told Moses to raise his staff over the water. Suddenly, a strong wind blew, and the sea split into two! The Israelites were able to walk across on dry ground.

When Pharaoh's army tried to follow, the waters came crashing back down, and they were swept away. The Israelites were safe! They saw that God had rescued them in an amazing way.

They celebrated by singing songs of praise, thanking God for His great power and love.

Key Lessons:

- God can make a way, even when things seem impossible.
- We should trust God instead of being afraid.
- God's power is greater than any problem we face.

Life Application:

Sometimes, we feel stuck in difficult situations, just like the Israelites. But this story teaches us that God always has a way to help us.

When we face problems, instead of being afraid, we should pray and trust that God is in control.

Reflective Questions/Exercises:

1. How do you think the Israelites felt when they saw the sea open?
2. What does this story teach you about trusting God?

3. Can you think of a time when God helped you through a problem?

Prayer:

Dear God,

Thank You for always making a way for Your people. Help me to trust You, even when things seem impossible. Remind me that You are always in control. Amen.

Lesson 11: Manna from Heaven – God Provides for His People

Study Scripture: Exodus 16:1-36

God Sends Food from the Sky

After God rescued the Israelites from Egypt, they traveled through the hot and dry desert. Soon, they ran out of food and began to complain to Moses. They were hungry and worried about what they would eat.

But God had a plan to take care of them. He told Moses that He would send food from heaven for them every day. The next morning, when the people woke up, the ground was covered with small white flakes. They called it "manna," which means "What is it?"

The manna was sweet and tasted like honey. Every morning, God provided fresh manna, and the Israelites gathered just enough for each day.

God also sent quail (small birds) in the evening for them to eat. Through this, God showed them that He would always provide for their needs.

Key Lessons:

- God always provides what we need.
- We should trust God instead of worrying.
- Being thankful is important when God blesses us.

Life Application:

Sometimes, we worry about what we don't have, just like the Israelites did. But this story reminds us that God always takes care of His children.

Instead of complaining, we should trust God to provide for us and always remember to be grateful for what He gives us.

Reflective Questions/Exercises:

1. How do you think the Israelites felt when they saw manna for the first time?
2. Why is it important to trust God for our needs?

3. How can you show gratitude for the things God gives you?

Prayer:

Dear God,

Thank You for always providing for me. Help me to trust You and not to worry. Teach me to be thankful for everything You give me. Amen.

Lesson 12: Jericho's Walls Fall – Victory Through Obedience

Study Scripture: Joshua 6:1-20

God's Unusual Battle Plan

After wandering in the desert for many years, the Israelites were finally ready to enter the Promised Land. But there was a big problem—the city of Jericho had high, strong walls, and no one could get inside.

Instead of using weapons to fight, God gave Joshua a special plan. He told Joshua and the Israelites to march around the city once a day for six days. They were not allowed to make a sound—just march and listen.

On the seventh day, they marched around seven times, and then the priests blew their trumpets.

Joshua told the people, "Shout! Because God has given us this city!"

As soon as they shouted, the walls of Jericho crumbled to the ground! The Israelites won the battle without fighting because they trusted and obeyed God's instructions.

Key Lessons:

- Obedience to God brings victory.

- God's ways are different from our ways.
- Faith requires trust, even when things don't make sense.

Life Application:

Sometimes, God asks us to do things that don't seem to make sense. But just like the Israelites, we must trust Him and follow His instructions.

When we listen to God, He gives us victory in our lives—not by our own strength, but by His power.

Reflective Questions/Exercises:

1. How do you think the Israelites felt when marching around the city?
2. Why is it important to follow God's instructions, even when they seem unusual?
3. What is something in your life where you need to trust God more?

Prayer:

Dear God,

Thank You for showing me that victory comes through trusting and obeying You. Help me to listen to Your instructions and to have faith in Your plans. Amen.

Lesson 13: Gideon's Small Army - Winning with God's Strength

Study Scripture: Judges 7:1-22

Gideon's Unlikely Victory

The Israelites were being attacked by a large and powerful enemy, the Midianites. They were afraid and needed help. God chose Gideon to lead an army to fight against them, but Gideon was unsure of himself.

At first, Gideon had 32,000 soldiers, but God told him, "You have too many men." So, God had Gideon send home anyone who was afraid. After that, only 10,000 remained.

But God said that was still too many! So, He told Gideon to take the soldiers to a stream for a water test. Only the men who drank water in a certain way were chosen to stay. In the end, Gideon was left with just 300 men!

Even though they were greatly outnumbered, Gideon trusted God. That night, each man carried a trumpet and a torch inside a jar. They surrounded the enemy's camp, blew their trumpets, smashed their jars, and shouted, "For the Lord and for Gideon!"

The Midianites became so confused and afraid that they ran away! God had won the battle for Gideon with only a small army.

Key Lessons:

- God's power is greater than any challenge we face.
- We don't need to be strong on our own—God fights for us.
- Even when we feel small or weak, God can use us for great things.

Life Application:

Sometimes, we feel like we're not strong enough or good enough to handle a problem. But Gideon's story shows us that God doesn't need big numbers or great strength—He just needs our trust and obedience.

When we feel afraid or unsure, we should remember that God is always bigger than any problem we face.

Reflective Questions/Exercises:

1. How do you think Gideon felt when God told him to reduce his army?
2. What does this story teach you about trusting God?
3. When have you felt small or weak? How can you trust God to help you in those times?

Prayer:

Dear God,

Thank You for showing me that I don't have to be the strongest or the best for You to use me. Help me to trust You in every situation and to remember that You fight my battles. Amen.

Lesson 14: Ruth's Loyalty – A Story of Love and Faithfulness

Study Scripture: Ruth 1:1-18

Ruth's Big Decision

A woman named Naomi lived in a faraway land with her husband and two sons. But one day, tragedy struck. Naomi's husband and sons passed away, leaving her and her two daughters-in-law, Ruth and Orpah, alone.

Naomi decided to return to her homeland, Bethlehem, and told Ruth and Orpah to stay behind and find new families. Orpah agreed and said goodbye, but Ruth refused to leave Naomi.

With deep love and loyalty, Ruth said, "Where you go, I will go. Your people will be my people, and your God will be my God."

Ruth and Naomi traveled to Bethlehem, where Ruth worked hard to provide food by gathering grain in the fields. She met a kind man named Boaz, who admired her faithfulness. Boaz later married Ruth, and together, they became part of God's special plan—Ruth became the great-grandmother of King David!

Key Lessons:

- Loyalty and kindness bring blessings.
- Faithfulness to family and God leads to great things.
- God rewards those who trust Him, even in difficult times.

Life Application:

Ruth's story reminds us that love, kindness, and faithfulness are important. Even when life is hard, we should choose to stay loyal to the people God has placed in our lives.

When we follow God's path, He will provide for us, just as He provided for Ruth.

Reflective Questions/Exercises:

1. Why did Ruth choose to stay with Naomi instead of going back home?
2. How does Ruth's story show us the power of faithfulness?

3. What is one way you can show kindness and loyalty to someone in your life?

Prayer:

Dear God,

Thank You for the story of Ruth, which teaches me about love and loyalty. Help me to be kind, faithful, and to trust in Your plan for my life. Amen.

Lesson 15: Samuel Listens to God's Voice

Study Scripture: 1 Samuel 3:1-10

God Speaks to Samuel

Samuel was a young boy who lived in the temple of God, serving under a priest named Eli. One night, while Samuel was sleeping, he heard a voice calling his name.

Thinking it was Eli, Samuel quickly ran to him and said, "Here I am! You called me." But Eli replied, "I didn't call you. Go back to bed."

This happened three times, and each time Eli told Samuel that he hadn't called him. Then, Eli realized that God was the one speaking to Samuel! He told Samuel, "The next time you hear the voice, say, 'Speak, Lord, for Your servant is listening.'"

When God called Samuel again, he answered just as Eli had instructed. From that day on, Samuel became a great prophet who listened to and spoke God's words.

Key Lessons:

- God speaks to us, and we must be ready to listen.

- Sometimes, we need guidance from others to understand God's voice.
- When we listen to God, He can use us for His great plans.

Life Application:

God may not always speak to us the way He spoke to Samuel, but He still guides us through His Word, prayer, and wise people in our lives.

It's important to listen carefully when God is leading us, whether through the Bible, our parents, or our teachers. When we listen, we grow closer to God.

Reflective Questions/Exercises:

1. Why do you think Samuel didn't recognize God's voice at first?
2. How can we listen to God in our lives today?
3. Who are some people in your life that help guide you in faith?

Prayer:

Dear God,

Thank You for speaking to me and guiding me in my life. Help me to listen carefully when You are teaching me something. Give me a heart that is ready to obey Your voice. Amen.

Lesson 16: David and Goliath – Defeating Giants with Faith

Study Scripture: 1 Samuel 17:1-50

A Shepherd Boy's Big Battle

The Israelites were at war with the Philistines, but the Philistines had a giant warrior named Goliath. He was over nine feet tall and wore heavy armor. Every day, he challenged the Israelites to send someone to fight him, but no one was brave enough.

A young shepherd boy named David came to visit his brothers in the army. When he saw Goliath mocking God and the Israelites, David was not afraid. He believed that God would help him defeat Goliath.

David refused to wear heavy armor or use a sword. Instead, he took his sling and picked up five smooth stones. He walked toward Goliath and declared that God would give him victory.

With one stone, David slung it toward Goliath's forehead, and the giant fell to the ground! The Israelites won the battle because David trusted in God instead of his own strength.

Key Lessons:

- With faith, even the biggest problems can be defeated.
- God gives us strength when we trust in Him.
- It's not about size or power—God looks at our hearts.

Life Application:

We all face giants in our lives—things that seem too big or scary to handle. It could be a difficult test, a problem at home, or feeling afraid.

Like David, we must remember that God is bigger than any problem we face. When we trust Him and stand strong, He will help us overcome challenges.

Reflective Questions/Exercises:

1. How do you think David felt when he saw Goliath?

2. Why did David trust God instead of being afraid?
3. What are some "giants" in your life, and how can you trust God to help you?

Prayer:

Dear God,

Thank You for reminding me that no problem is too big for You. Help me to trust You like David did and to be brave when I face challenges. I know that You will always be with me. Amen.

Lesson 17: Solomon's Wisdom – The Gift of Understanding

Study Scripture: 1 Kings 3:3-15

Solomon's Special Request

Solomon became king of Israel after his father, David. One night, God appeared to him in a dream and said, "Ask for whatever you want, and I will give it to you."

Solomon could have asked for money, fame, or a long life, but instead, he asked for wisdom so he could rule the people fairly and with understanding.

God was pleased with Solomon's choice. Because he didn't ask for riches or power, God not only gave him great wisdom but also blessed him with wealth, honor, and peace in his kingdom.

Solomon's wisdom became famous, and people from all over came to hear him give wise advice. His most famous decision was when two women came to him, both claiming to be the mother of the same baby. Solomon used his wisdom from God to find out the truth, and the real mother was revealed.

Key Lessons:

- True wisdom comes from God.
- God blesses those who seek understanding over selfish desires.
- Wisdom helps us make the right choices in life.

Life Application:

Every day, we have to make choices. Some are small, like what to eat or wear, but others are big, like how to treat people or how to solve problems.

Instead of only asking for things, we should pray for wisdom so that we can make good decisions and help others, just like Solomon did.

Reflective Questions/Exercises:

1. Why do you think Solomon asked for wisdom instead of riches or power?

2. How can you ask God for wisdom in your daily life?
3. What is a situation where you need wisdom to make the right choice?

Prayer:

Dear God,

Thank You for teaching me that wisdom is more valuable than riches. Help me to make good decisions and to listen when You guide me. Give me a heart that seeks to understand and do what is right. Amen.

Lesson 18: Elijah's Challenge - Fire from Heaven

Study Scripture: 1 Kings 18:16-39

Elijah's Bold Test of Faith

During the time of King Ahab, many people in Israel had turned away from the true God and started worshiping a false god named Baal. The prophet Elijah wanted to show them that only the Lord is real and powerful.

Elijah challenged 450 prophets of Baal to a test. They would each prepare a sacrifice and pray—the true God would send fire from heaven to burn the offering.

The prophets of Baal prayed all morning, shouting and dancing around their altar, but nothing happened. No fire came.

Then, it was Elijah's turn. He built an altar, placed the sacrifice on it, and even poured water all over it to make it harder to burn. Then, Elijah prayed to God.

Immediately, fire fell from heaven, burning up the sacrifice, the altar, and even the water! The people fell to the ground and shouted, "The Lord is God!" They saw with their own eyes that God is real and powerful.

Key Lessons:

- God is the only true God.
- Faith means trusting God even when others don't believe.
- God answers prayers in powerful ways.

Life Application:

Sometimes, people may try to convince us to follow the wrong path, just like Israel turned to Baal. But Elijah's story reminds us that God is the only one we should trust.

When we face challenges or doubts, we can pray to God and know that He will always show us the truth.

Reflective Questions/Exercises:

1. How do you think Elijah felt when he stood alone against the prophets of Baal?
2. What does this story teach us about trusting in God's power?

3. Have you ever prayed and seen God answer in an amazing way?

Prayer:

Dear God,

Thank You for showing us that You are the one true God. Help me to trust You, even when others don't. Give me courage to stand for what is right and to always believe in Your power. Amen.

Lesson 19: Elisha and the Widow's Oil – God's Abundant Blessing

Study Scripture: 2 Kings 4:1-7

A Widow in Need and God's Miracle

A poor widow came to Elisha, the prophet, because she was in great trouble. Her husband had died, and she had no money left. A man she owed money to wanted to take her two sons as payment for the debt.

The widow was desperate and didn't know what to do. Elisha asked her, "What do you have in your house?"

She replied, "I have only a little oil."

Elisha told her to borrow as many empty jars as she could from her neighbors. Then, he instructed her to pour her oil into the jars.

She did as Elisha said, and something amazing happened! The oil kept flowing and flowing, filling every jar until there were no more left.

Elisha told her to sell the oil, pay her debts, and live off the rest. Because of her faith and obedience, God provided more than she needed!

Key Lessons:

- God provides for those who trust Him.
- Even when we feel like we have little, God can multiply it.
- Obedience to God brings blessings.

Life Application:

Sometimes, we feel like we don't have enough—not enough money, strength, or even confidence. But this story shows us that God can take even the smallest things and turn them into great blessings.

Instead of focusing on what we lack, we should trust that God can provide in amazing ways.

Reflective Questions/Exercises:

1. How do you think the widow felt when her oil kept flowing?
2. What does this story teach you about trusting God?

3. Have you ever seen God provide for you or your family in a special way?

Prayer:

Dear God,

Thank You for always providing for my needs. Help me to trust You, even when things seem impossible. Teach me to be obedient and believe that You can do great things with what I have. Amen.

Lesson 20: Jonah and the Great Fish – Learning to Obey God

Study Scripture: Jonah 1-2

Jonah Runs Away from God

God gave Jonah an important mission—to go to the city of Nineveh and tell the people to stop doing wrong. But Jonah didn't want to go, so he ran away in the opposite direction!

He got on a ship, thinking he could escape from God. But suddenly, a huge storm shook the sea, and the sailors became afraid. Jonah realized that the storm was happening because he had disobeyed God.

Jonah told the sailors to throw him into the sea so the storm would stop. As soon as they did, the waters became calm. But instead of drowning, Jonah was swallowed by a giant fish!

Inside the fish's belly, Jonah prayed and asked for forgiveness. After three days, God made the fish spit Jonah out onto dry land. Jonah then obeyed God and went to Nineveh, where the people listened to his message and turned back to God.

Key Lessons:

- Running from God's plan brings trouble, but obedience brings blessings.
- God is always ready to forgive when we turn back to Him.
- No matter where we go, we can never hide from God.

Life Application:

Sometimes, we don't want to do what God asks us to do, just like Jonah. But when we try to run away, we only make things harder for ourselves.

Instead of resisting, we should trust that God's plans are always the best. And if we ever make a mistake, we can always pray and ask God to help us start again.

Reflective Questions/Exercises:

1. Why did Jonah try to run away from God?

2. What happened when Jonah finally obeyed God?

3. Have you ever disobeyed and later realized that listening to God was the best choice?

Prayer:

Dear God,

Thank You for always guiding me, even when I don't want to listen. Help me to obey You the first time and to trust that Your plans are good. When I make mistakes, remind me that I can always turn back to You. Amen.

Lesson 21: Daniel in the Lion's Den - God's Protection in Hard Times

Study Scripture: Daniel 6:1-23

Daniel's Faithful Prayer and the King's Command

Daniel was a faithful man who prayed to God every day. He worked for King Darius and was so wise and honest that the king trusted him more than anyone else.

Some jealous leaders didn't like this, so they tricked the king into making a new law: Anyone who prays to a god instead of the king will be thrown into a den of lions!

Even though Daniel knew about the law, he continued to pray to God just as he always did. The jealous leaders caught him and told the king.

The king didn't want to punish Daniel, but he had no choice. Daniel was thrown into a den full of hungry lions.

But that night, God sent an angel to shut the mouths of the lions! The next morning, the king ran to the den and called out, "Daniel, was your God able to save you?"

Daniel answered, "Yes! God protected me." The king was so amazed that he praised God and made a new law that everyone should worship the one true God.

Key Lessons:

- God protects those who remain faithful to Him.
- We should trust God, even when it's hard.
- Standing up for our faith can inspire others to believe in God.

Life Application:

Sometimes, doing the right thing isn't easy. We might face challenges, just like Daniel did. But we must stay faithful to God, knowing that He is always with us.

When we put our trust in God, He gives us courage and protects us, even in difficult times.

Reflective Questions/Exercises:

1. Why did Daniel continue to pray even when he knew about the king's law?
2. How do you think Daniel felt when he was thrown into the lion's den?

3. What are some ways you can stay faithful to God, even when it's hard?

Prayer:

Dear God,

Thank You for always protecting me. Help me to trust You and stand strong in my faith, just like Daniel did. Give me courage to do what is right, no matter what. Amen.

Lesson 22: The Fiery Furnace – Standing Strong in Faith

Study Scripture: Daniel 3:1-30

Three Friends Who Refused to Bow

In the land of Babylon, King Nebuchadnezzar built a huge golden statue and ordered everyone to bow down and worship it. Anyone who refused would be thrown into a fiery furnace.

Three men—Shadrach, Meshach, and Abednego—loved and worshiped only God. When the king's order was given, they refused to bow to the statue.

The king was furious! He told them, "If you don't bow, you will be thrown into the fire! What god can save you then?"

They replied, "Our God can save us. But even if He doesn't, we will never worship your statue."

The king was so angry that he ordered the furnace to be seven times hotter and had them thrown inside. But when the king looked into the fire, he was shocked!

Instead of three men, he saw four! The fourth man looked like a son of God. Shadrach, Meshach, and Abednego were walking in the fire unharmed!

The king called them out, and they came out without a single burn or even the smell of smoke. Seeing this miracle, the king praised God and made a new law that no one should speak against Him.

Key Lessons:

- True faith means standing strong, even when it's hard.
- God is always with us, even in the toughest moments.
- When we trust God, He can use our faith to show His power to others.

Life Application:

Sometimes, we are pressured to do things that go against our faith. It could be cheating, lying, or following the crowd. But this story teaches us that we must stand firm in what we believe, just like these three men did.

Even when life feels difficult, God is always with us, protecting and guiding us through the fire.

Reflective Questions/Exercises:

1. Why do you think Shadrach, Meshach, and Abednego refused to bow to the statue?
2. What does this story teach us about God's power and presence?
3. Have you ever had to stand up for what is right, even when it was difficult?

Prayer:

Dear God,
   Thank You for always being with me, even when

things are tough. Help me to stand strong in my faith and to trust You, just like Shadrach, Meshach, and Abednego did. Give me courage to do what is right. Amen.

Lesson 23: Queen Esther's Courage – Trusting God to Save Her People

Study Scripture: Esther 4:10-17

Esther's Brave Decision

Esther was a young Jewish woman who became queen of Persia without the king knowing she was Jewish. She lived in the palace, but outside the walls, her people were in danger.

A powerful man named Haman had convinced the king to sign a law to destroy all the Jewish people. Esther's cousin, Mordecai, begged her to go to the king and ask for help.

But there was a problem—no one could approach the king without being invited. If Esther went to him without permission, she could be put to death.

Mordecai reminded Esther, "Maybe you became queen for this very reason—to save your people!"

Esther knew she needed God's help. She asked all the Jews to pray and fast with her for three days. Then, she bravely went to the king.

Instead of punishing her, the king listened to Esther. She revealed Haman's evil plan, and the king saved the Jewish people from destruction.

Because of Esther's faith and courage, her people were rescued.

Key Lessons:

- God places us in the right place for a purpose.
- Courage means doing what's right, even when it's scary.
- Prayer gives us strength to face challenges.

Life Application:

Sometimes, we are afraid to speak up or do what's right because of what others might think. But Esther's story teaches us that God gives us courage when we trust Him.

When we face difficult decisions, we should pray and ask for God's guidance, just like Esther did.

Reflective Questions/Exercises:

1. Why was Esther afraid to go to the king?
2. What does this story teach us about trusting God in scary situations?

3. Have you ever had to stand up for someone or something important?

Prayer:

Dear God,

Thank You for Esther's courage and faith. Help me to be brave when I need to do what is right. Teach me to trust You and to remember that You have placed me where I am for a reason. Amen.

Lesson 24: Nehemiah Rebuilds Jerusalem's Walls

Study Scripture: Nehemiah 2:1-18

Nehemiah's Mission to Restore the City

Nehemiah was a Jewish servant to the king of Persia. One day, he heard that Jerusalem's walls had been destroyed, leaving the city unprotected. This news made him very sad.

Nehemiah prayed to God for help and asked the king for permission to go rebuild the walls. The king agreed and even sent supplies and soldiers to help him.

When Nehemiah arrived in Jerusalem, he saw how bad things were. But he didn't give up. He encouraged the people to work together and rebuild the walls.

Even though some enemies mocked and tried to stop them, Nehemiah and the people kept trusting God and working hard. In just 52 days, they finished rebuilding the walls, and Jerusalem was strong again!

Key Lessons:

- God helps us accomplish great things when we trust Him.
- Working together makes difficult tasks easier.
- We should not give up, even when facing challenges.

Life Application:

Sometimes, we face big challenges that feel impossible, just like Nehemiah did. But this story reminds us that with God's help, we can overcome obstacles.

Instead of giving up when things seem hard, we should pray, ask for help, and keep working toward our goals.

Reflective Questions/Exercises:

1. Why was Nehemiah sad when he heard about Jerusalem?
2. What does this story teach us about trusting God with big tasks?
3. Have you ever had to work hard to complete something? How did you feel when you finished?

Prayer:

Dear God,

Thank You for giving Nehemiah strength and wisdom to rebuild the walls. Help me to trust You when I face big challenges. Teach me to work hard, never give up, and rely on Your guidance. Amen.

Lesson 25: Job's Story – Faith and Patience Through Suffering

Study Scripture: Job 1:1-22

Job's Unshakable Faith

Job was a faithful man who loved and followed God with all his heart. He was also very blessed, with a large family, wealth, and good health.

But one day, Job's life changed completely. He lost his children, his livestock, and his health. He was covered in painful sores, and even his wife told him to give up on God.

Job's friends believed he had done something wrong to deserve this suffering, but Job knew he had been faithful. Even though he didn't understand why this was happening, he refused to turn away from God.

Later, God restored everything Job had lost, blessing him with even more than before. Through his suffering, Job learned that God's wisdom is greater than ours, and we must trust Him no matter what.

Key Lessons:

- Faith means trusting God even when life is hard.
- God's ways are higher than ours, even when we don't understand.

- Patience and faithfulness bring blessings in the end.

Life Application:

Sometimes, we go through difficult times that feel unfair. We may lose things we love or struggle with sadness. But Job's story teaches us that God is always in control, even when we don't understand His plan.

Instead of giving up, we should pray, trust God, and wait patiently, knowing that He has a purpose for everything.

Reflective Questions/Exercises:

1. How do you think Job felt when he lost everything?
2. What does this story teach us about trusting God in hard times?
3. Can you think of a time when you had to be patient and trust God?

Prayer:

Dear God,

Thank You for reminding me that You are always in control. Help me to trust You, even when life is difficult. Teach me to have patience and faith, just like Job. Amen.

Lesson 26: The Lord as Our Shepherd – God's Care for Us

Study Scripture: Psalm 23

God's Loving Care

King David wrote Psalm 23 to describe how God cares for His people, just like a shepherd cares for his sheep.

A shepherd guides, protects, and provides for his sheep. Without him, the sheep could get lost, hungry, or hurt. In the same way, God is our Shepherd. He leads us, provides for us, and keeps us safe.

Psalm 23 reminds us that God gives us peace, even in hard times. It says, "Even though I walk through the darkest valley, I will not be afraid, for You are with me." This means that even when we face difficulties, we don't have to fear—God is always with us.

Key Lessons:

- God lovingly takes care of us, just like a shepherd with his sheep.
- We don't have to be afraid because God is always with us.
- When we follow God, He leads us to good things.

Life Application:

Life can sometimes feel uncertain or scary. But Psalm 23 teaches us that God is always watching over us, guiding and protecting us.

Instead of worrying, we should trust in God's care, knowing that He loves us and will never leave us.

Reflective Questions/Exercises:

1. How does it make you feel to know that God is your Shepherd?
2. What does this psalm teach us about trusting God?
3. Can you think of a time when you felt God's protection in your life?

Prayer:

Dear God,
  Thank You for being my Shepherd and always taking care of me. Help me to trust You in every

situation and to remember that You are always by my side. Amen.

Lesson 27: God's Plan for Us – A Message of Hope from Jeremiah

Study Scripture: Jeremiah 29:11

God's Promise of a Good Future

The prophet Jeremiah spoke to the Israelites when they were feeling sad and hopeless. They had been taken far from their home into a foreign land, and they didn't know what would happen to them.

But God sent them a message of hope. He told them, "I know the plans I have for you—plans to give you a future and a hope."

Even though the Israelites were going through a difficult time, God wanted them to trust Him. He had a good plan for their future, even when they couldn't see it yet.

This promise isn't just for the Israelites—it's for us too! God has a purpose for our lives, and He is always working things out for our good.

Key Lessons:

- God has a special plan for each of us.
- Even in hard times, we can trust that God is in control.
- God's plans are always better than our own.

Life Application:

Sometimes, life doesn't go the way we expect. We might face challenges, disappointments, or changes that make us feel uncertain.

But God's promise in Jeremiah 29:11 reminds us that He has a good future planned for us. Even when we don't understand what's happening, we can trust that God is leading us in the right direction.

Reflective Questions/Exercises:

1. How does it make you feel to know that God has a plan for your life?
2. Why is it important to trust God, even when things don't go as planned?
3. Can you think of a time when something worked out better than you expected?

Prayer:

Dear God,

Thank You for having a good plan for my life. Help me to trust You, even when things don't go as I expect. Remind me that Your plans are always better than mine. Amen.

Lesson 28: Ezekiel's Vision – Life from Dry Bones

Study Scripture: Ezekiel 37:1-14

God's Promise to Bring Life Again

God gave the prophet Ezekiel a powerful vision. In the vision, God took Ezekiel to a valley full of dry bones. The bones represented God's people, who had lost hope and felt like they were forgotten.

Then, God asked Ezekiel, "Can these bones live again?" Ezekiel wasn't sure, but he knew that only God had the power to bring life.

God told Ezekiel to speak to the bones, and when he did, something amazing happened! The bones came together, and muscles and skin formed over them. But they still weren't alive.

Then, God told Ezekiel to speak to the breath, and when he did, the bones came to life and became a mighty army.

This vision was God's way of showing that He could bring new life and restore hope to His people, even when things seemed impossible.

Key Lessons:

- God can bring life and hope even in the darkest situations.
- Nothing is too hard for God—He can restore and renew us.

- When we feel lost or broken, God is always working to make things new.

Life Application:

There may be times when we feel hopeless, tired, or unsure about the future. But God has the power to renew us and bring new life into every situation.

When we trust in God, He can turn our struggles into strength and our worries into hope.

Reflective Questions/Exercises:

1. How do you think Ezekiel felt when he saw the dry bones come to life?
2. What does this story teach us about God's power to restore hope?
3. Have you ever experienced a time when God gave you strength when you felt weak?

Prayer:

Dear God,

 Thank You for reminding me that You can bring life and hope, even when things seem impossible. Help me to trust in Your power to renew and restore me. Amen.

Lesson 29: The Birth of Jesus – God's Greatest Gift

Study Scripture: Luke 2:1-20

The Savior is Born

A long time ago, God promised to send a Savior to the world. When the time came, a young woman named Mary was chosen to give birth to Jesus, the Son of God.

Mary and her husband Joseph traveled to Bethlehem for a census, but when they arrived, there was no room for them in the inn. They had to stay in a stable, where animals were kept.

That night, Mary gave birth to Jesus. She wrapped Him in swaddling cloths and laid Him in a manger.

Meanwhile, in a nearby field, shepherds were watching over their sheep. Suddenly, angels appeared, announcing, "Good news! A Savior has been born!" The shepherds hurried to Bethlehem and found baby Jesus lying in the manger.

They were filled with joy and praised God, knowing that the world's greatest gift had arrived.

Key Lessons:

- Jesus is the greatest gift that God has given us.
- God's promises always come true.
- We should share the good news of Jesus with others.

Life Application:

Christmas is not just about presents and decorations—it's about celebrating the birth of Jesus, our Savior.

We should always remember the true meaning of Christmas and take time to thank God for sending Jesus to bring us love, joy, and salvation.

Reflective Questions/Exercises:

1. Why was Jesus born in a stable instead of a palace?
2. How do you think the shepherds felt when they saw the angels?
3. What are some ways you can share the joy of Jesus' birth with others?

Prayer:

Dear God,
Thank You for sending Jesus as the greatest gift to the world. Help me to always remember

the true meaning of Christmas and to share Your love with others. Amen.

Lesson 30: Jesus the Good Shepherd – Caring for His People

Study Scripture: John 10:11-18

Jesus, Our Loving Shepherd

Jesus often used parables and stories to teach people about God's love. One of the most beautiful examples is when He called Himself "the Good Shepherd."

A shepherd's job is to take care of his sheep, leading them to food and water and protecting them from danger. The shepherd is willing to do anything to keep his sheep safe.

Jesus said, "I am the Good Shepherd. The Good Shepherd lays down His life for the sheep." This means that Jesus loves us so much that He was willing to give His life to save us.

Unlike a hired worker, who might run away when danger comes, Jesus never abandons His people. He knows each of us by name and is always guiding, protecting, and leading us toward what is best.

Key Lessons:

- Jesus cares for us just like a shepherd cares for his sheep.
- We can trust Jesus to guide and protect us.
- Jesus gave His life to save us because He loves us.

Life Application:

Sometimes, we may feel lost or unsure about life, just like sheep wandering without a shepherd. But Jesus reminds us that He is always with us, ready to guide us and keep us safe.

We should learn to listen to His voice, trust Him, and follow where He leads.

Reflective Questions/Exercises:

1. How does it make you feel knowing that Jesus is your Good Shepherd?
2. What does this story teach us about God's love and protection?
3. How can you follow Jesus more closely in your daily life?

Prayer:

Dear God,
   Thank You for sending Jesus to be my Good

Shepherd. Help me to trust in His guidance and follow His path. Remind me that I am never alone because You are always watching over me. Amen.

Lesson 31: Jesus Calms the Storm – Trusting Him in Difficult Times

Study Scripture: Mark 4:35-41

Jesus' Power Over the Storm

One evening, Jesus and His disciples got into a boat to cross a large lake. While they were sailing, a powerful storm suddenly appeared. Waves crashed into the boat, and water started filling it.

The disciples were terrified! But where was Jesus? He was asleep in the back of the boat.

The disciples woke Him up, shouting, "Teacher! Don't You care that we are about to drown?"

Jesus stood up and said to the storm, "Peace! Be still!" Immediately, the wind stopped, and the waves calmed down.

The disciples were amazed! Jesus asked them, "Why were you afraid? Do you still have no faith?"

Through this miracle, Jesus showed that He has power over everything, even the wind and sea.

Key Lessons:

- Jesus is in control, even when life feels stormy.
- We should trust Jesus instead of being afraid.
- Faith helps us stay calm, knowing that Jesus is always with us.

Life Application:

Sometimes, life feels like a storm. We face problems, fears, or challenges that make us feel like we're sinking. But just like Jesus was with the disciples in the boat, He is always with us, too.

Instead of panicking, we should pray, trust Jesus, and believe that He can bring peace to any situation.

Reflective Questions/Exercises:

1. How do you think the disciples felt when the storm suddenly stopped?
2. What does this story teach us about Jesus' power?
3. How can you trust Jesus more when you feel afraid or worried?

Prayer:

Dear God,

  Thank You for reminding me that You are in control of everything. When I feel afraid, help me to trust You and find peace, knowing that You are always with me. Amen.

Lesson 32: Feeding the 5,000 – Jesus Provides More Than Enough

Study Scripture: John 6:1-14

A Small Lunch Becomes a Big Blessing

One day, a huge crowd of over 5,000 people followed Jesus to listen to His teachings. After a long day, the people became hungry, but there was no food for them.

Jesus asked His disciples, "Where can we buy food for all these people?" But they had no money to buy so much food.

Then, a young boy offered his small lunch—just five loaves of bread and two fish. It wasn't much, but Jesus took the food, prayed over it, and started passing it out.

Amazingly, the food never ran out! Everyone ate until they were full, and when they collected the leftovers, there were 12 baskets of food left!

Jesus showed that He can take even the smallest offering and turn it into something great.

Key Lessons:

- God can multiply what we offer, no matter how small it seems.
- Trusting Jesus means believing He will provide for our needs.

- When we give generously, God can use it to bless others.

Life Application:

Sometimes, we may feel like we don't have much to give—whether it's our time, talents, or kindness. But this story reminds us that God can do great things with even the smallest offering.

Instead of holding back, we should give with a joyful heart and trust that God will provide for us and others.

Reflective Questions/Exercises:

1. How do you think the boy felt when he gave his small lunch to Jesus?
2. What does this story teach us about God's ability to provide?
3. How can you be generous and share what you have with others?

Prayer:

Dear God,

Thank You for reminding me that You can take something small and make it great. Help me to trust You to provide for my needs and to share what I have with others. Amen.

Lesson 33: The Lost Sheep – How God Searches for Us

Study Scripture: Luke 15:3-7

A Shepherd's Love for His Sheep

Jesus told a story about a shepherd who had 100 sheep. One day, one little sheep wandered away and got lost. Instead of thinking, "I still have 99, so it's fine," the shepherd left the 99 and went searching for the lost one.

He climbed hills, walked through valleys, and looked everywhere until he finally found the sheep. Overjoyed, he lifted it onto his shoulders and carried it home.

Then, he gathered his friends and celebrated, saying, "Rejoice with me! I have found my lost sheep!"

Jesus explained that this is how God feels about us. When we go astray, He never gives up on us. He searches for us and rejoices when we return to Him.

Key Lessons:

- God loves every person and never gives up on anyone.
- When we make mistakes, God welcomes us back with joy.
- Every person is valuable to God, no matter how lost they feel.

Life Application:

Sometimes, we may feel far from God because of mistakes or bad choices. But God never stops loving us. He is always ready to welcome us back with open arms.

If we see someone feeling lost, we should show kindness and remind them that God is always waiting for them.

Reflective Questions/Exercises:

1. Why do you think the shepherd searched for just one lost sheep?
2. How does this story show us God's love for us?
3. What can you do to help someone who feels lost or alone?

Prayer:

Dear God,
  Thank You for never giving up on me. When I

feel lost, help me to remember that You are always searching for me. Teach me to share Your love with others and to welcome them back, just like You do. Amen.

Lesson 34: The Good Samaritan – Showing Kindness to Everyone

Study Scripture: Luke 10:25-37

A Neighbor's Kindness

One day, a man asked Jesus, "Who is my neighbor?" To answer, Jesus told a parable about a man traveling on a dangerous road.

While walking, the man was attacked by robbers, beaten, and left on the ground. A priest came by but didn't stop to help. Then, a Levite (a religious leader) also passed by but ignored the injured man.

Finally, a Samaritan came along. The Samaritans and Jews did not get along, yet this Samaritan stopped to help. He bandaged the man's wounds, placed him on his donkey, and took him to an inn to rest.

Jesus asked, "Which of these three was a true neighbor?" The answer was clear—the Samaritan showed kindness, even when others didn't.

Jesus then said, "Go and do the same."

Key Lessons:

- Being a good neighbor means showing kindness to everyone.
- Helping others is more important than status or religion.

- True love is shown through action, not just words.

Life Application:

Sometimes, we see people who need help, but it's easier to walk away like the priest and the Levite. But Jesus wants us to be like the Good Samaritan—helping those in need, even if they are different from us.

We should love and care for everyone, not just those who are like us.

Reflective Questions/Exercises:

1. Why do you think the priest and Levite ignored the injured man?
2. How does this story show us the importance of kindness?
3. What are some ways you can be a good neighbor to someone in need?

Prayer:

Dear God,

Thank You for teaching me to love and help others. Give me a kind heart so I can care for people, even when it's not easy. Help me to be a good neighbor, just like the Good Samaritan. Amen.

Lesson 35: The Prodigal Son – God's Love and Forgiveness

Study Scripture: Luke 15:11-32

A Son Who Made a Big Mistake

Jesus told a parable about a father and his two sons. The younger son asked for his share of the family's money and left home to enjoy life.

At first, everything seemed great—he spent all his money on things he wanted. But soon, he had nothing left. A terrible famine came, and he was so hungry that he took a job feeding pigs.

One day, he realized his mistake. He thought, "Even my father's servants have food! I will go home and ask to be a servant."

As he walked home, his father saw him from far away. But instead of being angry, the father ran to him, hugged him, and forgave him. He even threw a big celebration because his son had returned.

The older brother was upset, but the father reminded him, "We must celebrate, because my son was lost, but now he is found!"

Key Lessons:

- God's love never runs out, even when we make mistakes.
- No matter how far we run, God is always ready to welcome us back.
- Forgiveness brings joy and restoration.

Life Application:

Sometimes, we make wrong choices and feel like we are too far from God. But just like the father in the story, God is always waiting for us with open arms.

Instead of staying away in shame, we should return to God, knowing that He will always forgive and love us.

Reflective Questions/Exercises:

1. Why did the younger son decide to go home?
2. How does this story show us God's love and forgiveness?
3. How can you practice forgiveness with others?

Prayer:

Dear God,
 Thank You for always loving me, even when I

make mistakes. Help me to turn back to You when I go the wrong way. Teach me to forgive others, just as You forgive me. Amen.

Lesson 36: Zacchaeus Meets Jesus – A Life Transformed

Study Scripture: Luke 19:1-10

A Man Who Wanted to See Jesus

Zacchaeus was a tax collector, and many people did not like him because he took extra money for himself. Even though he was rich, he felt something was missing in his life.

One day, Jesus came to Zacchaeus' town. Zacchaeus wanted to see Him, but he was too short to see over the crowd. So, he climbed a tree to get a better view.

When Jesus passed by, He stopped, looked up, and called Zacchaeus by name. He said, "Come down! I must stay at your house today."

Zacchaeus was shocked and excited! He welcomed Jesus into his home, and after spending time with Him, his heart changed. He decided to give back the money he had taken and help the poor.

Jesus said, "Salvation has come to this house today." Zacchaeus was no longer the same—his life was completely transformed by Jesus.

Key Lessons:

- Jesus sees and loves every person, no matter their past.

- When we truly meet Jesus, our hearts change.
- It's never too late to turn away from wrong and do what is right.

Life Application:

Sometimes, we feel unworthy because of past mistakes, but Jesus never ignores or rejects anyone. He sees us, knows us by name, and invites us to be close to Him.

When we allow Jesus to enter our hearts, He changes us for the better, just like He did for Zacchaeus.

Reflective Questions/Exercises:

1. Why do you think Zacchaeus was so eager to see Jesus?
2. How did meeting Jesus change Zacchaeus' life?
3. What can you do to show that your heart has been changed by Jesus?

Prayer:

Dear God,

Thank You for seeing me and loving me, no matter what. Help me to welcome You into my heart and to live a life that shows kindness, honesty, and love. Amen.

Lesson 37: Jesus Walks on Water – Faith Over Fear

Study Scripture: Matthew 14:22-33

Peter's Step of Faith

After a long day of teaching, Jesus sent His disciples ahead in a boat while He went up a mountain to pray. Later that night, a strong wind blew across the sea, and the disciples' boat was tossed by the waves.

Suddenly, they saw someone walking toward them on the water. They were terrified, thinking it was a ghost!

But Jesus called out, "Don't be afraid! It is I."

Peter, one of Jesus' disciples, wanted to test his faith. He said, "Lord, if it is You, let me walk on the water too." Jesus told him to come.

Peter stepped out of the boat and began walking on the water! But when he saw the strong wind and waves, he became afraid and started sinking.

He cried out, "Lord, save me!" Immediately, Jesus reached out His hand and pulled him up.

Jesus asked, "Why did you doubt?" When they got back into the boat, the wind stopped, and the disciples worshiped Jesus, realizing He was truly the Son of God.

Key Lessons:

- When we focus on Jesus, we can do things we never thought possible.
- Doubt and fear can make us sink, but Jesus is always there to help us.
- Faith means trusting Jesus even in the middle of life's storms.

Life Application:

Sometimes, life feels like a storm—things go wrong, and we feel afraid. But just like Peter, we must keep our eyes on Jesus instead of focusing on the problems around us.

Even when we struggle, Jesus is always there to lift us up and bring us back to safety.

Reflective Questions/Exercises:

1. Why do you think Peter was able to walk on water at first?
2. What made Peter start sinking?

3. How can you trust Jesus when facing challenges or fears?

Prayer:

Dear God,

Thank You for always being with me, even in the storms of life. Help me to keep my eyes on You and trust You completely. When I feel afraid, remind me that You are always ready to lift me up. Amen.

Lesson 38: Jesus Heals the Blind Man – Seeing Through Faith

Study Scripture: John 9:1-12

Healing a Man Who Couldn't See

One day, Jesus and His disciples saw a man who had been blind since birth. The disciples asked Jesus, "Why was this man born blind? Did he or his parents do something wrong?"

Jesus answered, "This happened so that God's power could be shown through him." Then, Jesus did something unusual—He spit on the ground, made mud, and spread it on the blind man's eyes.

Jesus told the man to go and wash in the Pool of Siloam. When he did, his sight was completely restored!

People were amazed and asked, "Is this the same man who used to beg?" Some believed it was a miracle, but others doubted. The healed man declared, "I was blind, but now I can see!"

Through this, Jesus showed that He not only heals physical blindness but also opens people's hearts to see the truth.

Key Lessons:

- Jesus has the power to heal both our bodies and our hearts.
- Faith allows us to see God's truth, even when others doubt.
- God's works are done to bring glory to Him.

Life Application:

Sometimes, we struggle to see what God is doing in our lives. We may feel confused, but just like the blind man, Jesus wants to open our eyes to His truth.

We must trust that God has a purpose for everything, even when we don't understand it right away.

Reflective Questions/Exercises:

1. Why did Jesus say the man was born blind?

2. How did the man show his faith in Jesus?
3. How can we trust Jesus to help us see His truth in our lives?

Prayer:

Dear God,

Thank You for opening my eyes to Your truth. Help me to trust You, even when I don't understand things. Let my faith be strong, and teach me to see the world through Your love. Amen.

Lesson 39: The Parable of the Talents – Using God's Gifts Wisely

Study Scripture: Matthew 25:14-30

A Lesson About Responsibility

Jesus told a parable about a man who went on a journey. Before he left, he gave his three servants different amounts of money (called talents).

- The first servant received five talents and worked hard to double them to ten.
- The second servant received two talents and also doubled them to four.
- But the third servant was afraid and hid his one talent in the ground.

When the master returned, he was happy with the first two servants because they had used their talents wisely. But he was disappointed with the third servant, who did nothing with what he was given.

Jesus used this story to teach us that God gives everyone special gifts, talents, and opportunities, and He wants us to use them for good.

Key Lessons:

- God gives us talents and expects us to use them wisely.
- Fear should not stop us from doing good things.
- When we use our gifts well, God blesses us with even more.

Life Application:

God has given each of us unique skills, talents, and opportunities. Some may be good at helping others, singing, drawing, or learning new things.

Instead of hiding our gifts, we should use them to serve God and help others.

Reflective Questions/Exercises:

1. Why was the master pleased with the first two servants?
2. What does this story teach us about using our talents?

3. What is one special gift or talent that you have, and how can you use it for good?

Prayer:

Dear God,

Thank You for giving me special talents and abilities. Help me to use them wisely, not hide them. Show me ways to bless others with what You have given me. Amen.

Lesson 40: The Last Supper – Jesus Prepares for His Sacrifice

Study Scripture: Luke 22:14-20

Jesus Shares a Special Meal

On the night before Jesus was arrested, He gathered His disciples for one last meal together. This meal became known as the Last Supper.

As they sat together, Jesus took bread, broke it, and gave it to His disciples. He said, "This is My body, given for you. Do this in remembrance of Me."

Then, He took a cup of wine and said, "This is My blood, poured out for many for the forgiveness of sins."

Jesus was telling His disciples that He was about to give His life to save people from their sins. This meal was a way to remember His great sacrifice.

After the meal, Jesus went to pray in the Garden of Gethsemane, preparing for what was about to happen.

Key Lessons:

- Jesus willingly gave His life to save us.
- We should remember and be thankful for Jesus' sacrifice.
- The Lord's Supper (Communion) helps us honor what Jesus did for us.

Life Application:

When we take part in Communion (the Lord's Supper), we are remembering Jesus' love and sacrifice.

Just like Jesus showed love, humility, and service to His disciples, we should live our lives with gratitude and kindness toward others.

Reflective Questions/Exercises:

1. Why did Jesus share this special meal with His disciples?
2. What does the bread and wine (or juice) represent in Communion?

3. How can we show thankfulness for Jesus' sacrifice in our daily lives?

Prayer:

Dear God,

Thank You for Jesus' sacrifice and for showing me how much You love me. Help me to always remember what He did and to live a life that honors Him. Amen.

Lesson 41: Jesus Prays in the Garden – Trusting God's Plan

Study Scripture: Matthew 26:36-46

A Moment of Deep Prayer

After the Last Supper, Jesus went to the Garden of Gethsemane with His disciples. He knew that the time had come for Him to suffer and die on the cross.

Feeling deep sorrow and pain, Jesus told His disciples, "Stay here and keep watch with Me." Then, He went a little farther and prayed to God.

Jesus prayed, "Father, if it is possible, take this suffering away from Me. But not My will, but Yours be done."

Even though Jesus was afraid, He trusted God's plan. When He returned, He found His disciples asleep instead of praying. He told them, "The time has come. I will be betrayed into the hands of sinners."

Shortly after, soldiers came and arrested Jesus. But He did not fight back—He was ready to follow God's plan.

Key Lessons:

- It's okay to feel afraid, but we must trust God's plan.
- Prayer gives us strength when we are struggling.
- Jesus chose to obey God, even when it was hard.

Life Application:

Sometimes, we face difficult situations that make us feel scared or uncertain. But Jesus' prayer reminds us that we can talk to God about our fears and ask for His strength.

Even when things don't go as we hope, God's plan is always for the best.

Reflective Questions/Exercises:

1. Why did Jesus pray in the garden before He was arrested?

2. What does this story teach us about trusting God's plan?
3. How can you pray when you are feeling scared or unsure?

Prayer:

Dear God,

Thank You for always being with me, even when I feel afraid. Help me to trust Your plan and to pray for strength like Jesus did. Teach me to follow You, even when it's difficult. Amen.

Lesson 42: The Crucifixion – Jesus' Ultimate Sacrifice

Study Scripture: Matthew 27:32-56

Jesus Gives His Life for Us

After Jesus was arrested, He was put on trial before the Roman governor, Pontius Pilate. Even though Jesus had done nothing wrong, the leaders wanted Him to be punished.

The soldiers mocked Jesus, placed a crown of thorns on His head, and made Him carry a heavy cross to a hill called Golgotha. There, they nailed Him to the cross and left Him to die.

Even in His pain, Jesus prayed for those who hurt Him, saying, "Father, forgive them."

At noon, darkness covered the land, and Jesus cried out, "It is finished!" Then, He bowed His head and died.

At that moment, the earth shook, the temple curtain tore in two, and people realized that Jesus truly was the Son of God.

Jesus' death was not the end. He gave His life to take the punishment for our sins, so that we could be saved.

Key Lessons:

- Jesus willingly gave His life to save us.

- His sacrifice shows God's deep love for us.
- Because of Jesus, we can be forgiven and have eternal life.

Life Application:

Jesus' crucifixion is the greatest example of love and sacrifice. Even when people were unkind to Him, He chose to forgive them.

Because Jesus died for us, we should live in a way that honors Him—showing love, kindness, and forgiveness to others.

Reflective Questions/Exercises:

1. Why did Jesus allow Himself to be crucified?
2. What does Jesus' sacrifice teach us about God's love?
3. How can we show gratitude for what Jesus did for us?

Prayer:

Dear God,
 Thank You for sending Jesus to die for my sins.
Help me to always remember His sacrifice and to
live a life that honors You. Teach me to love and
forgive others, just as Jesus did. Amen.

Lesson 43: The Resurrection – Jesus Defeats Death

Study Scripture: Matthew 28:1-10

Jesus Rises from the Dead

After Jesus was crucified, His body was placed in a tomb, and a large stone was rolled in front of it. Soldiers guarded the tomb to make sure no one could take His body.

Three days later, early in the morning, some women went to visit the tomb. But when they arrived, they found the stone rolled away!

An angel appeared and told them, "Do not be afraid! Jesus is not here—He has risen, just as He said!"

The women were filled with joy and excitement. As they ran to tell the disciples, Jesus appeared to them! He greeted them and said, "Do not be afraid. Go and tell My brothers that I am alive."

Jesus' resurrection proved that He is more powerful than death and that He truly is the Son of God.

Key Lessons:

- Jesus conquered death, giving us the hope of eternal life.

- We can trust Jesus because He always keeps His promises.
- The resurrection is the greatest victory in history!

Life Application:

Because Jesus rose from the dead, we can have hope and joy. Even when life is difficult, we know that God's power is greater than any problem we face.

Jesus' resurrection also reminds us that we have the gift of eternal life with God if we trust in Him.

Reflective Questions/Exercises:

1. How do you think the women felt when they found the empty tomb?
2. What does Jesus' resurrection mean for us today?
3. How can we share the joy of Jesus' victory with others?

Prayer:

Dear God,

 Thank You for raising Jesus from the dead and giving us hope. Help me to live with joy, knowing that You have defeated sin and death. Teach me to share this good news with others. Amen.

Lesson 44: The Great Commission – Sharing the Good News

Study Scripture: Matthew 28:16-20

Jesus' Final Instructions

After Jesus rose from the dead, He spent time with His disciples, teaching them and preparing them for what was next.

One day, He took them to a mountain and gave them a special command. He said, "Go and make disciples of all nations, baptizing them in the name of the Father, the Son, and the Holy Spirit. Teach them to obey everything I have commanded you."

This was Jesus' Great Commission—His mission for all His followers. He wanted them to spread

His message of love and salvation to the whole world.

Jesus also gave them a promise: "I am with you always, to the very end of the age." Even though they had a big job to do, they would never be alone.

Key Lessons:

- Jesus calls all of us to share His message with others.
- We don't have to be afraid—Jesus is always with us.
- The Good News of Jesus is for everyone, everywhere.

Life Application:

Sometimes, we may feel shy or unsure about telling others about Jesus. But the Great Commission reminds us that sharing His love is part of our purpose.

We can share Jesus' message through our words, our actions, and by being a good example. Even small acts of kindness can help spread God's love.

Reflective Questions/Exercises:

1. Why did Jesus tell His disciples to share the Good News with all nations?

2. What does Jesus' promise—"I am with you always"—mean to you?

3. How can you share Jesus' love with someone this week?

Prayer:

Dear God,

Thank You for giving me a purpose and a mission. Help me to share Your love and truth with others. Give me courage to speak about You and remind me that You are always with me. Amen.

Lesson 45: Jesus Ascends to Heaven – The Promise of His Return

Study Scripture: Acts 1:6-11

Jesus Returns to Heaven

After Jesus rose from the dead, He spent 40 days with His disciples, teaching them about God's kingdom and preparing them for their mission.

One day, He took them to a hill and gave them an important message: "You will receive power when the Holy Spirit comes on you, and you will be My witnesses to the ends of the earth."

Then, as they watched, Jesus began to rise into the sky! A cloud covered Him, and He disappeared from their sight.

The disciples stood there, amazed. Then, two angels appeared and said, "Why are you looking at the sky? Jesus will return in the same way you saw Him go!"

Jesus had gone back to heaven, but His promise remained—one day, He will come back.

Key Lessons:

- Jesus is alive and reigning in heaven.

- He promised to return for His followers.
- We should live every day ready for His return.

Life Application:

Even though Jesus is not physically on Earth, we can still feel His presence in our hearts and through the Holy Spirit.

Instead of just waiting for His return, we should live in a way that honors Him, sharing His love and doing good in the world.

Reflective Questions/Exercises:

1. How do you think the disciples felt when they saw Jesus ascend into heaven?
2. What does Jesus' promise to return mean to you?
3. How can you live in a way that prepares for His return?

Prayer:

Dear God,

   Thank You for the promise that Jesus will return. Help me to live in a way that pleases You, sharing Your love and truth with others. Give me faith to trust in Your timing. Amen.

Lesson 46: The Holy Spirit Comes – God's Power for Believers

Study Scripture: Acts 2:1-13

The Day of Pentecost

After Jesus ascended to heaven, He told His disciples to wait in Jerusalem for a special gift—the Holy Spirit.

On the day of Pentecost, the disciples were gathered in a room when suddenly, a loud sound like a rushing wind filled the house. Then, flames of fire appeared over each person's head, and they were filled with the Holy Spirit!

Immediately, they began to speak in different languages. People from many nations were in Jerusalem, and they were amazed, saying, "How are they speaking in our languages?"

Peter stood up and explained, "This is what Jesus promised! The Holy Spirit has come to give us power to share God's message with the world."

That day, thousands of people believed in Jesus and were baptized. The Holy Spirit had arrived, giving power and boldness to Jesus' followers.

Key Lessons:

- The Holy Spirit gives us strength and guidance.
- God's power helps us share the Good News with others.
- When we trust in Jesus, the Holy Spirit is always with us.

Life Application:

Sometimes, we feel afraid or unsure about sharing our faith. But the Holy Spirit gives us courage, wisdom, and strength to live for Jesus.

We may not see flames of fire, but the Holy Spirit is still working in us today, guiding us and helping us make the right choices.

Reflective Questions/Exercises:

1. How do you think the disciples felt when the Holy Spirit came?

2. What does this story teach us about God's power?
3. How can you rely on the Holy Spirit in your daily life?

Prayer:

Dear God,

Thank You for sending the Holy Spirit to guide and strengthen me. Help me to listen to Your voice and have the courage to share Your love with others. Fill me with Your power and wisdom. Amen.

Lesson 47: Peter and John Heal a Lame Man – The Power of Jesus' Name

Picture Prompt:

Study Scripture: Acts 3:1-10

A Miracle at the Temple Gate

One day, Peter and John were on their way to the temple to pray. At the temple gate, they saw a lame man who had been unable to walk since birth. He sat there every day, begging for money because he could not work.

When he saw Peter and John, he asked them for money. But instead of giving him coins, Peter looked at him and said, "Silver or gold I do not have, but what I do have I give you. In the name of Jesus, walk!"

Then, Peter took the man by the hand, and instantly, his legs became strong! He jumped up, walked, and began praising God!

Everyone who saw him was amazed. They had known him as the man who could never walk, but now, he was leaping with joy!

Peter told the crowd that this miracle happened because of Jesus' power.

Key Lessons:

- **Jesus' name** has power to heal and restore.
  - God's blessings are greater than material things like money.
  - When God does something amazing, we should praise Him.

Life Application:

This story reminds us that Jesus' power is still at work today. Even when we don't receive exactly what we ask for, God gives us what we truly need.

Instead of only focusing on physical needs, we should also pray for spiritual strength, healing, and faith.

Reflective Questions/Exercises:

1. How do you think the man felt when he was healed?

2. Why did Peter say, "In the name of Jesus, walk"?

3. What is something you can praise God for today?

Prayer:

Dear God,

Thank You for the power of Jesus' name. Help me to trust in You and remember that Your blessings are greater than anything money can buy. Teach me to always praise You for what You do in my life. Amen.

Lesson 48: Saul's Conversion – A Life Transformed by Jesus

Study Scripture: Acts 9:1-19

Saul Encounters Jesus

Saul was a man who hated Christians and wanted to stop them from spreading the message of Jesus. He even arrested and hurt believers because he thought he was doing the right thing.

One day, as Saul was traveling to Damascus to capture more Christians, a bright light from heaven flashed around him. He fell to the ground and heard a voice say, "Saul, Saul, why are you persecuting Me?"

Saul asked, "Who are You, Lord?" and the voice replied, "I am Jesus, whom you are persecuting."

When Saul got up, he was blind! His friends led him into the city, where he fasted and prayed for three days.

Then, a man named Ananias came to him, placed his hands on him, and said, "Jesus has sent me so you may see again and be filled with the Holy Spirit."

Immediately, something like scales fell from Saul's eyes, and he could see again! He was baptized and became a follower of Jesus.

Saul, who once hated Christians, became one of the greatest messengers of the Gospel. His name was later changed to Paul, and he spent the rest of his life teaching about Jesus.

Key Lessons:

- Jesus can change anyone's heart, no matter their past.
- God's grace is powerful and available to all.
- When we follow Jesus, our lives should be transformed.

Life Application:

Saul's story reminds us that no one is too far from God's love. No matter what mistakes we've made, Jesus can change our hearts and give us a new purpose.

When we accept Jesus, our lives should reflect His love and truth, just like Paul's did.

Reflective Questions/Exercises:

1. How do you think Saul felt when he heard Jesus speak to him?
2. What does this story teach us about God's power to change lives?
3. How can you show that Jesus has transformed your life?

Prayer:

Dear God,
   Thank You for Your grace and the power to change hearts. Help me to follow You completely

and let my life be a testimony of Your love. Teach me to share Your truth with others. Amen.

Lesson 49: Paul and Silas in Prison – Singing in the Storm

Study Scripture: Acts 16:16-34

Singing in Chains

Paul and Silas were preaching about Jesus when some people got angry and had them arrested and beaten. They were thrown into prison, with their feet locked in chains.

Instead of complaining, Paul and Silas began praying and singing hymns to God. Even though they were suffering, they praised God with joy.

At midnight, something amazing happened—a violent earthquake shook the prison! The doors flew open, and the chains fell off every prisoner.

The jailer woke up and was afraid that all the prisoners had escaped. But Paul called out, "Don't harm yourself! We are all still here."

The jailer was amazed. He asked, "What must I do to be saved?" Paul and Silas told him, "Believe in the Lord Jesus, and you will be saved."

That night, the jailer and his whole family believed in Jesus and were baptized.

Key Lessons:

- We can worship God even in difficult situations.
- God's power can set us free—physically and spiritually.
- When we trust God, our faith can inspire others to believe in Him.

Life Application:

Sometimes, life feels unfair, and we go through hard times. But Paul and Silas remind us that we should praise God no matter what happens.

When we trust God in the middle of struggles, He can turn our difficulties into opportunities to help others find Him.

Reflective Questions/Exercises:

1. Why did Paul and Silas sing and pray instead of complaining?

2. What happened when they trusted God in prison?

3. How can you praise God even when life is difficult?

Prayer:

Dear God,

Thank You for reminding me that I can trust You in all situations. Help me to praise You, even when things are hard. Let my faith inspire others to know You. Amen.

Lesson 50: The New Heaven and New Earth – God's Eternal Promise

Study Scripture: Revelation 21:1-7

God's Perfect Future

The Bible ends with an amazing promise—one day, God will make everything new!

In a vision, John saw a new heaven and a new earth. He saw a holy city, the New Jerusalem, coming down from God. A loud voice declared, "God's home is now among His people! He will wipe away every tear, and there will be no more death, sorrow, or pain."

John also saw something incredible—God Himself sitting on the throne, saying, "I am making everything new!"

In this new world, there will be no suffering, no sin, and no darkness—only joy, love, and the presence of God forever.

This is God's promise to all who believe in Him. One day, we will live in a perfect home with Jesus, where everything is good forever.

Key Lessons:

- God has prepared a perfect future for His children.
- There will be no more pain, sadness, or death in heaven.
- We can look forward to spending eternity with Jesus.

Life Application:

Sometimes, life on earth is hard, but this promise reminds us that something greater is coming. We can have hope and joy, knowing that God has prepared a perfect place for those who love Him.

Until that day, we should live for Jesus, sharing His love and helping others to know Him.

Reflective Questions/Exercises:

1. How does God's promise of a new heaven and earth give us hope?

2. What do you think heaven will be like?

3. How can we live in a way that prepares us for God's perfect future?

Prayer:

Dear God,

Thank You for preparing a beautiful and perfect place for us. Help me to live with hope, knowing that You are making all things new. Teach me to share Your love so that more people can be part of Your eternal kingdom. Amen.

Conclusion

Over the past 50 lessons, we have gone on an exciting journey through the Bible, learning about God's love, power, and promises. From the creation of the world to the promise of a new heaven and earth, we have seen how God's plan has always been about love, redemption, and hope.

Through stories of faithful men and women, miracles, and Jesus' teachings, we have discovered that God is always with us, guiding, protecting, and providing for His people. No matter our circumstances, He calls us to trust Him, obey His Word, and share His love with others.

This Bible study has reminded us that:

- God is our Creator, and He has a plan for each of us.
- Faith in God gives us strength in difficult times.

- Jesus' life, death, and resurrection bring us salvation.
- The Holy Spirit guides us to live in truth and righteousness.
- Heaven is our eternal home, and we should live in a way that honors God.

As we conclude this study, let us not forget the lessons we have learned. The Bible is not just a collection of stories—it is God's living Word, meant to guide and shape our lives.

May we continue to:

■ Read and study God's Word daily
■ Pray and seek His wisdom in all things
■ Share His love with others
■ Trust in His promises and live for Him

The journey of faith does not end here—it continues every day as we walk with Jesus. May we always grow in our love for God and follow Him with all our hearts.

Final Prayer:

Dear God,

Thank You for teaching me through Your Word. Help me to remember everything I have learned and to live in a way that honors You. Fill my heart with love, faith, and courage as I continue my journey with You. Guide me each day, and let my life be a light for others. In Jesus' name, Amen.